475

NEVERTHELESS

NEVERTHELESS

BY MARIANNE MOORE

THE MACMILLAN COMPANY · NEW YORK

Designed by Stefan Salter

Manufactured in the United States of America by H. Wolff, New York

With the exception of NEVERTHELESS which appeared in *Contemporary Poetry* (entitled IT IS LATE, I CAN WAIT), THE WOOD-WEASEL which appeared in *The Harvard Advocate*, and ELEPHANTS which appeared in *The New Republic*, these poems were published by *The Nation*.

CONTENTS

NEVERTHELESS

NEVERTHELESS

you've seen a strawberry
    that's had a struggle; yet
    was, where the fragments met,

a hedgehog or a star-
    fish for the multitude
    of seeds. What better food

than apple-seeds—the fruit
    within the fruit—locked in
    like counter-curved twin

hazel-nuts? Frost that kills
    the little rubber-plant-
    leaves of kok-saghyz-stalks, can't

harm the roots; they still grow
    in frozen ground. Once where
    there was a prickly-pear-

leaf clinging to barbed wire,
    a root shot down to grow
    in earth two feet below;

as carrots form mandrakes
    or a ram's-horn root some-
    times. Victory won't come

to me unless I go
    to it; a grape-tendril
    ties a knot in knots till

knotted thirty times,—so
  the bound twig that's under-
  gone and over-gone, can't stir.

The weak overcomes its
  menace, the strong overcomes itself. What is there

like fortitude! What sap
  went through that little thread
  to make the cherry red!

THE WOOD-WEASEL

emerges daintily, the skunk—
don't laugh—in sylvan black and white chipmunk
regalia. The inky thing
adaptively whited with glistening
goat-fur, is wood-warden. In his
ermined well-cuttlefish-inked wool, he is
determination's totem. Out-
lawed? His sweet face and powerful feet go about
in chieftain's coat of Chilcat cloth.
He is his own protection from the moth,

noble little warrior. That
otter-skin on it, the living polecat,
smothers anything that stings. Well,—
this same weasel's playful and his weasel
associates are too. Only
WOOD-weasels shall associate with me.

ELEPHANTS

Uplifted and waved until immobilized
wistarialike, the opposing opposed
mouse-gray twined proboscises' trunk formed by two
trunks, fights itself to a spiraled inter-nosed

deadlock of dyke-enforced massiveness. It's a
knock-down drag-out fight that asks no quarter? Just
a pastime, as when the trunk rains on itself
the pool it siphoned up; or when—since each must

provide his forty-pound bough dinner—he broke
the leafy branches. These templars of the Tooth,
these matched intensities, take master care of
master tools. One, sleeping with the calm of youth,

at full length in the half dry sun-flecked stream-bed,
rests his hunting-horn-curled trunk on shallowed stone.
The sloping hollow of the sleeper's body
cradles the gently breathing eminence's prone

mahout, asleep like a lifeless six-foot
frog, so feather light the elephant's stiff
ear's unconscious of the crossed feet's weight. And the
defenseless human thing sleeps as sound as if

incised with hard wrinkles, embossed with wide ears,
invincibly tusked, made safe by magic hairs!
As if, as if, it is all ifs; we are at
much unease. But magic's masterpiece is theirs,—

Houdini's serenity quelling his fears.
Elephant ear-witnesses-to-be of hymns
and glorias, these ministrants all gray or
gray with white on legs or trunk, are a pilgrims'

pattern of revery not reverence,—
the centuries-old carefullest unrehearsed
religious procession without any priests,
play. Blessed by Buddha's Tooth, the obedient beasts

themselves as toothed temples blessing the street, see
the white elephant carry the cushion that
carries the casket that carries the Tooth.
Amenable to what, matched with him, are gnat

trustees, he does not step on them as the white-
canopied blue-cushioned Tooth is augustly
and slowly returned to the shrine. Though white is
the color of worship and of mourning, he

is not here to worship and he is too wise
to mourn,—a life-prisoner but reconciled.
With trunk tucked up compactly—the elephant's
sign of defeat—he resisted, but is the child

of reason now. His straight trunk seems to say: when
what we hoped for came to nothing, we revived.
As loss could not ever alter Socrates'
tranquillity, the elephant has contrived

equanimity. With the Socrates of
animals as with Sophocles the Bee, on whose
tombstone a hive was incised, sweetness tinctures
his gravity. His held up fore-leg for use

as a stair, to be climbed or descended with
the aid of his ear, expounds the brotherhood
of creatures to man the encroacher by the
small word with the dot, meaning know,—the verb bùd.

These knowers, these distinct rememberers
like Bùd, of what they have experienced, are
"unable to pierce by one dart from the bow
four plaintain-leaves laid at the points of a square;"

and cannot, like Buddha, change missiles to wreaths,
alter their shape, bisect hairs in the dark, make
their wisdom apparent in rays of all hues,
or turn heat, exasperated, to earthquake-

fire. Yet they "arouse the feeling that they are
allied to man" and can change roles with their trustees.
Hardship makes the soldier; then teachableness
makes him the philosopher—as Socrates,

prudently testing the suspicious thing, knew
the wisest is he who's not sure that he knows.
Who rides on a tiger can never dismount;
asleep on an elephant, that is repose.

Note: For data incorporated in the above stanzas I am in-
debted to a lecture-film entitled Ceylon, the Won-
drous Isle by Charles Brooke Elliott. And Cicero
deploring the sacrifice of elephants in the Roman
Games, said they "aroused both pity and a feeling
that the elephant was somehow allied with man—"
(p. 52, Animals for Show and Pleasure in Ancient
Rome by George Jennison).

A CARRIAGE FROM SWEDEN

They say there is a sweeter air
        where it was made, than we have here;
        a Hamlet's castle atmosphere.
At all events there is in Brooklyn
something that makes me feel at home.

Noone may see this put-away
        museum-piece, this country cart
        that inner happiness made art;
and yet, in this city of freckled
integrity it is a vein

of resined straightness from north-wind
        hardened Sweden's once-opposed-to-
        compromise archipelago
of rocks. Washington and Gustavus
Adolphus, forgive our decay.

Seats, dashboard and sides of smooth gourd-
        rind texture, a flowered step, swan-
        dart brake, and swirling crustacean-
tailed equine amphibious creatures
that garnish the axle-tree! What

a fine thing! What unannoying
        romance! And how beautiful, she
        with the natural stoop of the
snowy egret, gray-eyed and straight-haired,
for whom it should come to the door,—

of whom it reminds me. The split
 	pine fair hair, steady gannet-clear
 	eyes and the pine-needled-path deer-
swift step; that is Sweden, land of the
free and the soil for a spruce-tree—

 	vertical though a seedling—all
 	needles: from a green trunk, green shelf
 	on shelf fanning out by itself.
The deft white-stockinged dance in thick-soled
shoes! Denmark's sanctuaried Jews!

The puzzle-jugs and hand-spun rugs,
 	the root-legged kracken shaped like dogs,
 	the hanging buttons and the frogs
that edge the Sunday jackets! Sweden,
you have a runner called the Deer, who

when he's won a race, likes to run
 	more; you have the sun-right gable-
 	ends due east and west, the table
spread as for a banquet; and the put-
in twin vest-pleats with a fish-fin

effect when you need none. Sweden,
 	what makes the people dress that way
 	and those who see you wish to stay?
The runner, not too tired to run more
at the end of the race? And that

cart, dolphin-graceful? A Dalgrén
 	light-house, self-lit?—responsive and
 	responsible. I understand;

it's not pine-needle-paths that give spring
when they're run on, it's a Sweden

of moated white castles,—the bed
    of densely grown flowers in an S
    meaning Sweden and stalwartness,
skill, and a surface that says
Made in Sweden: carts are my trade.

THE MIND IS AN ENCHANTING THING

is an enchanted thing
   like the glaze on a
katydid-wing
      subdivided by sun
      till the nettings are legion.
Like Gieseking playing Scarlatti;

like the apteryx-awl
   as a beak, or the
kiwi's rain-shawl
      of haired feathers, the mind
      feeling its way as though blind,
walks along with its eyes on the ground.

It has memory's ear
   that can hear without
having to hear.
      Like the gyroscope's fall,
      truly unequivocal
because trued by regnant certainty,

it is a power of
   strong enchantment. It
is like the dove-
      neck animated by
      sun; it is memory's eye;
it's conscientious inconsistency.

It tears off the veil; tears
        the temptation, the
mist the heart wears,
            from its eyes,—if the heart
            has a face; it takes apart
dejection. It's fire in the dove-neck's

iridescence; in the
        inconsistencies
of Scarlatti.
            Unconfusion submits
            its confusion to proof; it's
not a Herod's oath that cannot change.

IN DISTRUST OF MERITS

Strengthened to live, strengthened to die for
    medals and position victories?
They're fighting, fighting, fighting the blind
    man who thinks he sees,—
who cannot see that the enslaver is
enslaved; the hater, harmed. O shining O
       firm star, O tumultuous
          ocean lashed till small things go
      as they will, the mountainous
      wave makes us who look, know

depth. Lost at sea before they fought! O
    star of David, star of Bethlehem,
O black imperial lion
    of the Lord—emblem
of a risen world—be joined at last, be
joined. There is hate's crown beneath which all is
       death; there's love's without which none
         is king; the blessed deeds bless
      the halo. As contagion
        of sickness makes sickness,

contagion of trust can make trust. They're
    fighting in deserts and caves, one by
one, in battalions and squadrons;
    they're fighting that I
may yet recover from the disease, My

Self; some have it lightly, some will die. "Man's
        wolf to man" and we devour
                ourselves. The enemy could not
            have made a greater breach in our
                defenses. One pilot-

ing a blind man can escape him, but
        Job disheartened by false comfort knew
that nothing can be so defeating
        as a blind man who
can see. O alive who are dead, who are *paradox*
proud not to see, O small dust of the earth
                that walks so arrogantly,
                    trust begets power and faith is
                an affectionate thing. We
                    vow, we make this promise

to the fighting—it's a promise—"We'll
        never hate black, white, red, yellow, Jew,
Gentile, Untouchable." We are
        not competent to
make our vows. With set jaw they are fighting,
fighting, fighting,—some we love whom we know,
            some we love but know not—that
                hearts may feel and not be numb.
                It cures me; or am I what
                    I can't believe in? Some

in snow, some on crags, some in quicksands,
        little by little, much by much, they
are fighting fighting fighting that where
        there was death there may

be life. "When a man is prey to anger,
he is moved by outside things; when he holds
             his ground in patience patience
                    patience, that is action or
                 beauty," the soldier's defense
                    and hardest armor for

the fight. The world's an orphans' home. Shall
         we never have peace without sorrow?
without pleas of the dying for
      help that won't come? O
quiet form upon the dust, I cannot
look and yet I must. If these great patient
             dyings—all these agonies
                    and woundbearings and bloodshed—
              can teach us how to live, these
                 dyings were not wasted.

Hate-hardened heart, O heart of iron,
         iron is iron till it is rust.
There never was a war that was
         not inward; I must
fight till I have conquered in myself what
causes war, but I would not believe it.
      I inwardly did nothing.
         O Iscariotlike crime!
      Beauty is everlasting
            and dust is for a time.